The Greatest Wisdom Ever Written

Lao Tzu's Tao Te Ching Explained Like Never Before

Table of contents

Introduction:

The Tao Te Ching is an 81 verse text written approximately 2500 years ago by Lao Tzu, who is the central figure of Taoism. Though the text uses mysterious language, it is packed full of the deepest wisdom and is considered by hundreds of millions of people to be the greatest teaching on wisdom, spirituality and enlightenment ever to be written.

Over the years I have heard and read from many people discussing the Tao Te Ching and have noticed time and time again that the deeper and more profound truths Lao Tzu attempts to teach are often misunderstood or missed altogether. To be able to understand the Tao you must come to understand the true nature of reality and your self.

In this book I work my way through many significant verses of the Tao Te Ching and explain the true meaning behind Lao Tzu's words. I also explain the philosophical or spiritual realisations necessary to understand and embody these teachings.

Due to copyright concerns I do not actually include the verses of the Tao Te Ching in this text, I only number each verse and talk about them one at a time. I allow you to reference your own copy of whichever of the popular translations you prefer to read. I keep a few of these popular translations in mind when I write, but any version you choose to read will work fine as they are all only different words translating the same teaching which goes beyond words.

 I am a meditation, wisdom and life coach, I offer teachings both online and in person.

Anyone who wishes to contact me seeking inexpensive teachings can do so through my email: allpurpose2134@gmail.com

You can also take a look at my other books on Amazon.

Verse One Of The Tao Te Ching

The Tao Te Ching starts off by saying that the Tao cannot be described in words. Words can never be a true or full reflection of the Tao. This is because the Tao is the infinite, it is reality itself, which can only be understood through personal experience. Any words attempting to describe reality itself will always fall short or mislead.

Lao Tzu then says that using words, labels and names is actually the mother of or the origin of the ten thousand things. What he is trying to say here is that the Tao, reality itself, is actually made up of one essence. Any attempts to differentiate between different parts of the Tao and label these parts is actually creating these differences which did not exist before you tried to separate them. A good way to understand ultimate reality is to have an empty mind. Reality and your mind are the very same thing, they are of the same essence. With an empty mind there is no process of labelling things going on, and all the appearances which arise in the mind appear as one image or one experience which is constantly changing and passing away, it is all undifferentiated and there is no attachment. On the other hand, by distinguishing between certain appearances and trying to name them you are actually causing all these new distinctions and divisions to become real. By doing so you are leaving behind the Oneness of unity with the Tao, of awareness of the truth, and instead entering a state of worldliness, desire and confusion with thousands of things to consider, including making distinctions between the "self" and "other" people.

Lao Tzu then says that desire is what blinds you to the spiritual mystery of life. When you are caught up in desire you are living a life of egotism and selfishness. Your mind is focused on chasing pleasures or avoiding dissatisfaction, it is concerned with the mortal perspective and the conditions of the world. Whereas when you are freed from the bondage of desire then your mind is not concerned with such petty things, but is instead focused on what is truly important in life; spiritual understanding and God.

Verse Two Of The Tao Te Ching

In this verse Lao Tzu talks about the dependence that opposites such as good and bad have in terms of their meaning. Many people make the mistake of focusing too much on the opposite nature of these examples and perhaps believe this verse is simply a reference to dualism and how opposites create each other. It goes much deeper than that. Lao Tzu is actually giving a teaching on the dependent origination of all things and the lack of inherent existence or inherent meaning in all of reality, he is talking about emptiness.

He teaches that even things such as beauty only exist dependently, which means that they depend on other ideas to have any meaning at all, and so they do not really exist on their own, they are empty of inherent or independent meaning. Lao Tzu is attempting to strip away the most base beliefs that you have stored in your mind which have created your false idea of a conditioned world, he is trying to empty your mind of all attachment to concepts by helping you to realize that even spacial distinctions such as high and low are only ideas. He takes this teaching further by demonstrating that distinction making and meaning making is not only happening with your visual judgements such as beauty and ugliness, but is even occurring for time itself, such as before and after. It is the ideas in our mind which make us believe in all these things. Ideas arise simultaneously with our experiences leading us to have pre-conditioned ideas of what is what and what is true. With an empty mind that resides in a present awareness of the Tao, there is nothing left but the perfection of spiritual unity and you can see the truth undistorted by ideas.

This is why the wise one who has realised the truth doesn't care for talking or achieving, for gaining possessions or trying to take credit for things. One who lives in reality sees that all things are arising and disappearing so he isn't attached to anything and his actions reflect that freedom.

Verse Three Of The Tao Te Ching

This verse begins with Lao Tzu explaining that desire and attachment is the cause of strife and an unsettled way of life. Without desire and attachment then there is no need to fight for positions of praise or power, and there will be no greed or separation causing stealing of valuable possessions.

Lao Tzu then makes it clear that his wise man's intention is literally to empty people's minds of knowledge because he knows knowledge often distorts spiritual understanding and complicates the pure and simple. By ridding your mind of so many beliefs, concepts, attachments, preconceived notions, and conditioned ideas, you are also ridding your self of delusions, arrogance, misplaced authority, pride, narcissism, ego-identification, and other destructive habits. In modern times people are so heavily conditioned by certain ideas, such as an egotistical 'patriotic' idea of which country they identify with, that they are controlled by these ideas and even willing to hate or go to war with other countries. Even the notion that there is such a thing as separate countries is a result of the over-complication that attachment to ideas causes. Lao Tzu makes it clear that those who think that they know often have harmful focuses in life and are disconnected from the harmony that comes with wisdom. He suggests that the desire to act itself is not aligned with true wisdom. This is because wanting to take action usually means thinking that there is something wrong with the world, or that there is the desire to change things, which indicates a lack of understanding of the impermanent and divine nature of the dream-like experience which makes up our lives. Desiring to change the world is like desiring to change the shape of water, any appearance of success will soon be shown to have been false, as water will always follow its natural rhythm of fluidity, as will the Tao.

Verse Five Of The Tao Te Ching

Here Lao Tzu makes it clear that the wise man ought to act just like the Tao. That he ought to live in accordance with the principals of the Tao. This is because the Tao is really the authentic, true self. The Tao doesn't distinguish between people or judge them, and nor should you. Your unfiltered nature is actually the core of perfect wisdom and virtue. The truly virtuous person recognises that all other people are the same as him, so why would he reject any one? He recognises that all people are really just transient manifestations of the Tao, so why would he be attached to them?

The Tao is described as empty yet capable of issuing forth endless manifestations from itself. The way to understand this is to look into your own mind. Your inner mind is completely empty, if you look into it you will feel and see nothing, it appears to be empty of any substance or meaning. Yet it is capable of always producing, endlessly creating new manifestations, ideas, visions, dreams, thoughts, experiences and forms, though all of these are empty too. You, God, The Tao, The Universal Mind, are all just meaningless words for the same ultimate reality which is beyond words. The Tao is the incomprehensible totality of reality, but it is all just "mind" or "spirit", exactly like your own, that is how you can know it intimately. You are never disconnected from the Tao, you have never lost your oneness with it, at worst your true nature is only ever distorted by delusions and attachments. The very act of being attached to something automatically implies separation from it. For there to be attachment there must be someone who is attached and something that they are attached to. As long as you are attached to anything you cannot be at one with all things. In other words, as long as you are focused on one object that is arising in your mind you cannot be presently aware of your whole mind-experience.

Verse Thirteen Of The Tao Te Ching

Caring for the possibility of either favor or disgrace are equally bad for you because this demonstrates that you are attached to the outcome of your position in the world and the worldly conditions you experience. Most of what happens in the world is completely outside of your control, so being attached to the way the story plays out is illogical and dangerous. It will cause you so much suffering to be at the mercy of an unpredictable and transient life. You will feel great anxiety and fear, always worrying about what will happen to you, or you will feel endless longing and agitation as you try to gain your desires. Do you really want to experience all this pain just because you hope to eventually reach a better life? Isn't it better to end the pain now by accepting reality as it is? If you see your body as your self then you are bound to experience a lot of suffering and anxiety. Not only will you fear death and have the regrets of a mortal perspective, but you will also be concerned with unnecessary things like your personal appearance or achievements.

The body is not your self-substance, it is just another transient form arising in this experience of life, like any other fleeting form, such as thoughts or dreams, the body will disappear too, yet the spirit or mind that is really you will remain unaffected. If you can put a stop to the delusional belief that your body is your self-substance then you can also be free of the fear and existential anxiety which is always plaguing your mind and preventing your spirit from acceptance, peace and being at rest. Recognise that the entire world is also just a manifestation of Tao and that all you know of it is really just arising within you and therefore is you. For you, there is nothing else that can be known but your own mind as far as you are concerned. If you can perceive all things as your own self, then you will be free from desire, envy, hate, and fear of others.

Verse Fifteen Of The Tao Te Ching

Here Lao Tzu speaks of the qualities of the ancient masters of the Tao. He describes them as careful and cautious. The reason a wise man would be careful and cautious is because he is always aware of the complexity of life and the widespread impacts of even minor actions. The master has a deep understanding of the infinite nature of causality and how every action in the world can effect everything else. For example, something you say today might still be quoted thousands of years from now and effect the way the world turns out. Similarly, everything you do or say to others has a causal ripple effect which alters many other outcomes. *Butterfly effect!*

To understand the infinite nature of causality you should perceive that every object in the room is a piece of the causality of the world. Each piece of causality cannot exist on its own, instead, a thing always arises simultaneously and dependently with other things. A house or the idea of a house cannot exist without walls, doors, and so on. So there is really no such thing as a house that has inherent or independent existence. As Lao Tzu described earlier, this is true for all ideas and concepts, including beauty and even time. It is by relation to other things that meaning exists. It is by contrast with other things that definition exists, and it is because of the infinite chain of interdependent causality that the world exists. Becoming aware of your impact on the chain of causality is a humbling and awesome experience. You gain a true understanding of your importance as you realise that you are truly capable of making a huge difference that will effect every other living being in the world. Even the tone of voice with which you use to communicate to others can effect the outcome of people's entire lives, that is how important your actions are, and that is why the ancient masters were so careful and cautious. Although their minds were empty and present, they still maintained an awareness of the complex and infinite Tao. Having a true awareness of the Tao means being connected to truth itself. All wisdom, insight, understanding and virtue is naturally granted to the one who is connected to the Tao. So even while being completely present, the masters were deeply aware of all the possibilities of life, so they understood the importance and significance of all things and the need to remain focused.

The reason the masters were reserved like guests is because they were humble. They did not presume to be in control of the world, so they did not try to assert power over it or think that they could direct everything. You are only a guest of the world, it is not your permanent dwelling, that is why the masters acted like humble guests. They were not attached to the outcome of their life and accepted the flow of things, that is why they were like unseasoned wood that has not yet been fashioned.

This verse then goes on to describe that the way to settle something which is troubled, or to clear that which is confused, is to gain clarity through patience. Being patient allows all the stirred up mud to settle down so that you can see clearly. It allows all the confusing aspects of life, such as riled up emotions, or the pressure of the moment, to fade away so that you can have an unblocked vision of how things really are. This same principal of the revealing power of patience applies to taking action. Usually you will find that you are in a state of agitation and restlessness. Your mind is often thinking about what's next or trying to rush even the most simple of tasks. Even while washing your hands you might find yourself rushing to dry them and move on! This state of restlessness and agitation indicates that you are not in acceptance of the present moment. It is important to learn to accept whatever you are doing. This is the only way to live in the reality of the now. This verse of the Tao Te Ching urges you to let stillness and rest become your core condition, and that way you will know when and how to act without being rushed. Whenever you are rushed or pressured you are actually just being dragged along by the conditions of life and you are not really free. Only by slowing your life down will you be able to find a state of rest and freedom of direction. Patience truly is one of the greatest virtues.

Lao Tzu then advises that the master who cherishes the reason of the Tao does not seek to fulfil his desires. If you are seeking to become fulfilled that means that you are not yet fulfilled and are not at rest. Longing, desire and being in a state of anticipation are actually forms of suffering. Mental suffering is almost always the result of imagination of the past or future or due to an imagined idea that something is "lacking" or absent. The reality is that "absence" does not really exist, it is just an abstract idea that you are "missing" something. Be present and look around you right now. Look around the room. Is there any suffering in that room? Is anything really "lacking" in that room? No? Then where is the suffering coming from? It's only arising due to your fantasies and thoughts. If you are seeking then you are suffering. Stop seeking and start accepting. This is a good habit you must practice over and over again if you want it to become your natural state.

Verse Sixteen Of The Tao Te Ching

Here Lao Tzu teaches that all things are in a state of rising and returning, and promotes the return to the root of all things. The return to the source of life, which is heaven and the eternal.

If you are immersed in the world and have forgotten your eternal and divine root then you are disconnected from heaven and an awareness of your eternal life. Not knowing that life is eternal is the cause of so much chaos and evil. If someone believes that they only have one life to live then they are much more likely to be selfish, greedy, stressed, desirous, unsatisfied, impatient, fearful and so on. Whereas if you know that life is eternal, what is there to fear? What reason would there be to rush? There would be no reason to desire anything when you know that all things will eventually come to you, and then disappear in accordance with destiny.

Greater even than an awareness of eternity is the actual experience of being at one with the source, of entering heavenly states. This is an experience which is attained through deep meditation, it is very insightful and powerful, though it is not a necessary experience for enlightenment to occur since it is still just transient, so you should not become attached to it. Through deep meditation your ego, thoughts and bodily sensations eventually fade away completely until you feel, think and see nothing of your illusory worldly identity. Heaven is found deep within your mind, that is where the kingdom of God resides, or more accurately, it is found at the core of reality itself. The experience of egolessness is extremely freeing. You realize that you are not bound to anything. That you do not have a body, and that you are not attached to the world. It is a merging with the infinite void and it is a very blissful and peaceful experience of understanding that you are one with God, capable of anything yet not needing to seek to fulfil any desires. The actual experience is like floating in the dark emptiness of your inner mind while being fully aware of the light of the living eternal spirit and experiencing a feeling of great elation and freedom. Anyone who doubts their divine origins can find the truth for themselves by engaging in deep meditation until their ego eventually dissolves and they experience this heavenly state.

Verse Twenty Of The Tao Te Ching

Lao Tzu tells us that learning is the cause of our troubles and anxiety. What he means is that knowledge of the world is often a curse that limits your freedom and in many different ways complicates the pure and simple nature of your existence. Without thinking about knowledge of the world your mind remains in its natural state of emptiness and freedom, like the freshness of a child's mind. By thinking about the world you suddenly put a great weight on your shoulders. All sorts of troublesome concerns arise out of thin air. There are now duties to perform, people to fear, survival issues to worry about, unsolvable problems, so many things to desire, and a huge world full of millions of people and places. How could you not feel anxiety hearing about such overwhelming things that you could never possibly grasp all of?

Though you are one with the infinite God, you are not at this moment experiencing infinite things, you never could and were not meant to try and learn all of this. The manifestations of the mind of God are all empty, dream-like experiences. None of them are permanent or enduring, they are more like an infinite stream of mirages or illusions. Not only can learning about them become a confusing burden, but it is also in essence a delusional thing to do. Besides enlightened wisdom, all other knowledge is provisional. At each moment your mind is either empty or only capable of thinking about one thing at a time, it can really only know one thing at a time. If you are honest with yourself you will realize that you really don't know much at all. So someone who believes they know a lot or is trying to learn a lot is deluding themselves. It is like trying to store water in a bag with a hole in it as it all pours out. It is also fostering further attachment to the world, which takes away from the more important spiritual focus.

Another reason that learning causes problems and anxiety is because it implies learning from others. Lao Tzu is not talking about self-knowledge and wisdom, which is already within you, he is talking about the knowledge other people tell you. Hearsay is often subjective or untrue. People have many illogical or inaccurate beliefs which can easily confuse you and mislead you. Even the most basic and simple things that you've been told are true can be seen as completely wrong from the enlightened perspective. It is always better to learn and grow by living than it is to be told what to believe or how to act. Freedom and wisdom can only be achieved independently, no one can give you spiritual growth.

Lao Tzu then goes on to describe his rare and exclusive qualities which are a result of his enlightenment. His way of life is shown to be completely opposite to ordinary people's lives. He is not emotional, not attached to a home, wanders about freely, has no desires, and even seems like he is dull and stupid. How is it that this wise way of life seems to completely contradict all of our natural inclinations? Don't we naturally want to be comfortable, fulfil our desires, express our emotions, and make use of our intelligence? The reason the wise master is so different is because he does what ordinary people don't do, he values God rather than the temporary creations of God.

He has set his aim higher than the mortal life of pleasure and suffering, he is instead aiming for the spiritual life of heaven and bliss. He has recognized that the egotistical life of personhood is filled with suffering, agitation and turmoil, so he has abandoned it completely. Even if we know this is the true and wise thing to do, most of us are not brave enough to do this. We are afraid of the consequences. We are afraid of discomfort, afraid of death, afraid of not having a secure future, and afraid of losing the things we desire. The truth is that we are like cowardly, lazy addicts. We have become addicted to a lower form of existence, it is the only thing we find familiar, and though it is often not so bad, like all addiction, it is a short sighted way of life that we will come to regret.

Remaining in the world of desire keeps us ignorant and makes us want to ignore the facts of life, such as that we are all, very soon, going to die and will not be able to take anything with us when that time comes. We won't be able to take our home, our desires, our comfort, our loved ones, or any of the things we are attached to with us beyond this life. We are foolishly attempting to store up all our treasures, knowledge and achievements in a temporary safe that will soon dissolve. On the other hand, in Lao Tzu's case, he is storing up his treasures and his knowledge in a permanent safe, he is focused on eternity, on God, on heaven, on living in accordance with the way of the Tao. He knows that all things will fade away so he doesn't condition himself to be reliant on anything. He is practising a way of life which is based on the truth and not on illusions. He is creating good karma, which is the continued energy of one's habits, so that he can benefit from it forever. He has chosen the Tao as his refuge because it is the only real refuge, even if it is an unpopular choice and doesn't win us our desires in this short life. Lao Tzu has found independent comfort in his mind, so he is comfortable despite good or bad fortune, his comfort comes with him wherever he goes and is not reliant on anything. He has found a permanent home in his inner being, so he is at home no matter where he goes. He has fulfilled his greater spiritual desire, so he experiences bliss without relying on any sensory pleasures. He has secured eternal life beyond death, so he has nothing to fear.

It is up to each of us to overcome our delusional addiction to the comforts of this one worldly life so that we can rise to transcendental states of being. You can ween yourself off of your addictions by learning to discipline your mind through practicing meditation and non-desire diligently. Bravely enter more and more deeply into your inner being and you will start to see that there is something much greater which awaits you, a way of life without misery or feelings of meaninglessness. Does this mean you have to become homeless and abandon everything? No! Radical abandonment actually demonstrates too much of a belief in the story of the person. What you should do is change your focus away from the little self, the ego, toward freedom, wisdom, independence, the inner mind, the infinite and the eternal. Have faith and don't feel pressured, as Lao Tzu said, the journey of a thousand miles begins with a single step.

Verse Twenty Seven Of The Tao Te Ching

Here Lao Tzu teaches that the wise man always saves, helps and teaches people, regardless of whether they are deemed "bad" or outcast. He recognises the value in all people, and he has seen the importance of teaching them. This is a very significant lesson, it not only teaches unconditional forgiveness and compassion, but it also reveals a very important truth, which is that the inclination to teach the truth to others is profoundly spiritual. It is part of your core spiritual drive to desire to tell the truth, it is a manifestation of your divinity, it is actually one of the only true meaningful things to do in life. This desire to spread truth is so powerful that sometimes it will be all that matters to you. Think about how you feel when there is a truth left unspoken and you want people to know it, it is like an itch you need to scratch. Think about when someone has told lies about you, and you want to inform others of the truth, that desire will be so powerful that you will barely be able to sleep at night. Think about when you see other people speaking or acting ignorantly, you will want nothing more than to show them the truth for the benefit of all.

You should take this lesson very seriously, it is the secret to finding true fulfilment and purpose in this worldly life. Your true inner passion, a passion which will never fade, is to tell the truth to others, because your inner being knows that the truth has the power to heal all problems and to turn the world into a paradise, you know that it is in your benefit and the benefit of everyone else to hear it. There are a lot of lies that people tell each other, especially in modern society. It is almost like entire cultures are built on lies and deceptions, and so whole populations of people lead insane lives and have very distorted values. People's hearts have become so hardened that they shut their minds off from the truth and purposefully try to avoid contemplating it. The more you see this tragedy the more you will realise that your purpose is to know the truth yourself, and then use it to help set others free. Once you are awakened to the truth yourself you will never be satisfied with remaining silent about it, you will always want to share it with others. The truth includes all that is necessary to heal the world, such as virtues like compassion and forgiveness, and thus can bring the world to a state of harmony and good sense. Nothing else is needed.

Verse Thirty Of The Tao Te Ching

In this verse Lao Tzu warns us against the use of force and violence and tells us how these are never a solution to any problem. In today's world force and the threat of violence are used to control just about every aspect of society. They are used to limit food distribution, to make sure land is paid for, to maintain the law, to sue others for money, to punish people in an attempt to stop crime, and much more. The entirety of modern civilisation is built around the use of force and the threat of violence, but the consequences of this are dire. The problem with using these methods is that there is no end to all this violence, because violence perpetuates violence. There is never the possibility for things to get better. The ideal of a more perfect world is crushed and there is no hope for one because, as Lao Tzu teaches, you cannot use force or violence without there being negative effects. You cannot teach people to become more wise or compassionate with force and violence, it is impossible. Idealism, optimism and virtue have no chance to thrive because the very fabric of our society is held together with pessimism, distrust and vice. This sad reality has a very negative effect on the mental health of all people who live under its grip. It causes people to be greedy, to be afraid of each other, to be separate and divided, to seek to persecute each other, to struggle alone, and to generally be depressed about the lack of a better future to look forward to. Humanity cannot prosper as long as people have a base-line automatic distrust of each other. It is like people treat each other as guilty of bad character until proven innocent. Most people feel that it is a hopeless effort to try and improve the world because the rules we live under will never allow humanity to flourish. People have been conditioned by this insane way of life for so long that they don't believe there is any other way to live.

Lao Tzu teaches that this way of life is not in harmony with the Tao, and that which is not in harmony with the Tao will inevitably come to destruction. The Tao is a creative spirit which is endlessly expressing new manifestations with complete freedom. To try to condition the world to remain stale, rigid and hard is not following the Tao. To try to keep people under the oppression of misplaced and immoral authority, or to dominate their lives and tell them how to act, is all completely opposite to the way of the Tao. The wise man recognises the core principals and qualities of the divine spirit and tries to align himself with them, so that he can be one with God. The Tao creates and allows its creations to be free, it manifests beings but doesn't cling to them or believe that it has authority over them.

There is no arrogance in the spirit. Therefore the holy man, which is the man who believes in good and strives for it, never tries to dominate people. He doesn't try to force the direction of destiny, which would only be a futile effort ending in disappointment. He accepts things as they are and does not try to force his own idea of what is good, he doesn't try to mould the world based on his desires because he knows the nature of goodness is eternal and unchanging. Trying to control things only serves to complicate them and leads you to a dull exhausting state of being which is not really living. Instead of creating conflict when there is a disagreement you should always be the one to yield, because you have recognised that living in peace and with love is infinitely more valuable than getting your way.

Verse Thirty Three Of The Tao Te Ching

In this verse Lao Tzu tells us that there is a very big difference between knowing others or conquering others, and knowing yourself or mastering yourself. Knowing others may bring you worldly intelligence and the strength to conquer others, but it cannot bring you enlightenment or true value. When we come to know others we are only analysing or judging the outward appearances and actions of people, which provides shallow, surface knowledge. Such knowledge usually leads us to become arrogant and think that we are better than others, because we often tend to focus on the flaws that people have. When we conquer others we are only dominating through force of power or intelligence, but this never leads us to gain anything of inherent value. When we see others we are only ever seeing their bodies or their actions, which are only temporary manifestations of the Tao. On the other hand knowing yourself means diving deeply into your inner mind and becoming intimately familiar with the way of the Tao. Knowing yourself is the only way to gain any true wisdom, all else that we learn from others is hearsay and ideology which cannot lead us to recognition of our eternal nature. Within you are the answers to all the questions you have, you simply have to empty your mind and ask your inner being what the truth is and you will see that you already know everything that is truly important.

If you're able to master yourself, that is the greatest achievement. Mastering your own mind means you can be free of all the negative mental aspects which constantly arise in you, such as agitation, depression, dissatisfaction, anxiety, regret, and so on. It is not an easy thing to master yourself, so don't make the mistake of thinking that it is achieved simply by having the correct beliefs. To master yourself you have to practice disciplining your mind and repeatedly clearing it of impurities such as emotional instability. These impurities actually take away your free will because you become a slave to so many invading negative thoughts, imaginary conversations, or mental loops and habits that you can't escape from. This is why it is all-important to engage in regular meditation, there is nothing more serious. Later Lao Tzu makes it clear that he understands that you may be reluctant to do take this path, and I will get to that topic when it arises in the Tao Te Ching.

Here Lao Tzu also teaches that contentment is true wealth. Why wait for the wealth the world has to offer? If you're waiting to gain it, at what point will you say that you have enough? Gain control of your mind and settle it, let it be content in the present moment by ending its tendency to always be clinging, then you have gained a richness that will never leave you.

At the end of this verse Lao Tzu urges you to not to fail in your spiritual progression in this life, so that when death comes you are ready and have achieved everlasting life. This is achieved simply through habit. Remember that the habits of your mind and the energy those create is called your karma, which is all that follows you after this life. For example, if you allow yourself to be angry then that will cause future anger. If you allow yourself to be sad then that will cause future sadness. If you give in to your desires then that will cause future temptation to do so again. It is very simple. In the same way, if you direct your mind to follow the habits of egolessness, self mastery, presence, and meditation, then this good karma will follow you at death, so that you are not subject to the process, but instead become the master of it. To be with ego means to be attached to your body and identity. To be egoless means to be unattached and at one with awareness of the flow of life. If you are egoless, aware, and in control of your mind when death comes, then you will not again become re-attached to any illusions.

Verse Thirty Eight Of The Tao Te Ching

The most significant part of this verse that I want to explain is where Lao Tzu describes how the man possessing the qualities of the Tao, the master, does nothing and doesn't feel a need to do anything. On the other hand Lao Tzu says that the man who doesn't possess a high level of wisdom is always doing things and always feels the need to be doing.

This is a vital teaching, it reveals the mental slavery which is caused by restlessness and delusion. Most people are always doing things, they simply cannot stop. From the moment they get up in the morning to the moment they go to sleep at night, day after day, they move from one distraction or task to the next, always keeping their minds busy, and often experience concern over missing out on the things life has to offer. It is like they are caught in a loop of endless activity or a headlong rush and cannot slow down. If such a person tries to stop engaging in activity and mental activity for even a few minutes, such as attempting meditation, they cannot do it. They will begin fidgeting, feeling restless, feeling agitated, and will soon go back to distracting themselves. It is like they are mad and cannot control themselves, they are much like a child that has an attention disorder, at least when it comes to paying attention to their own minds. If they are paying attention to some sensory pleasure like television, then they can focus for hours, but when it comes to paying attention to their inner activity, it is like someone has set them on fire! They can barely stand it, as if they were in real unbearable pain or were trying to grasp hold of something slippery and hot. Most people find it hard to pay attention to their own minds for more than a few moments at a time before becoming highly agitated, and some people will not even try to do this once in their entire lives. Imagine living for decades and never once taking a day to try to understand how your own mind works! It is completely absurd, but this is a very revealing truth to realize.

It reveals the insanity of the egotistical person, the person who is attached to the body and the world, the person without mental discipline. You might notice that you have this same trouble, and it is very serious, so you shouldn't ignore that it is indeed a problem. This compelling restlessness is like being a slave to your own mind. If you exist only in this hurried state of life there is no true rest. If you become aware of yourself while in this state you will observe that it is as if you are being dragged along by the circumstances of your life with no control. Moving from one task to the next endlessly. Acting and reacting, only trying to satisfy desires and survival needs, as if your mind is some kind of highly unstable machine that needs constant maintenance to maintain its comfort. You have likely been caught in this condition of existence for many lifetimes, endlessly exerting effort through your body, thoughts and words. When is enough ever going to be enough?

This is why enlightenment is referred to as liberation or freedom, it is because you have been in a mental prison for lifetimes, repeating the same mistakes, continuously trying to satisfy desires and then becoming dissatisfied again, never making the spiritual progression which is necessary to rise above the ego. It is as if you have been blindly trapped in a dream this whole time. The things that have been keeping you from awakening are ignorance, beliefs, delusion, attachment, desire, narrow mindedness, longing, and all of the vices such as laziness, lust, greed, anger, and hate.

no desire = Peace !

The one who is in the bondage of desire always feels the need to be doing things, but the wise the one has already achieved contentment and freedom, he is not lacking anything, so he doesn't feel the need to act. His actions arise authentically and freely, they are not forced upon him by his unstable feelings. This is the teaching of the importance of stillness.

Verse Thirty Nine Of The Tao Te Ching

In this verse Lao Tzu speaks a lot about unity, oneness, harmony and holism. An important teaching to take away from this verse is the wisdom of holism and holistic thinking. It is vital that we learn to see the whole rather than having a narrow, limited perspective. When we consider anything from a limited point of view we are never able to understand what is really happening, and we are not able to deal with it accordingly. This wisdom is critical when it comes to problems and solutions. There is usually not just a single cause to a problem, and the same is true for solutions. If we try to approach a problem thinking only of patching up the most obvious cause, we will likely only mitigate the issue and cause other problems to arise. This happens very often in society, especially when it comes to solving problems on the political and governmental level, and it demonstrates how narrow minded most people are in their thinking. For example, when it comes to the problem of people stealing, using copyright, unfair trades, damaging someone's business, reputation or property. The narrow minded solution which has been implemented by the government is to encourage people to sue each other to regain their losses. This perfectly demonstrates the idiocy of trying to help a situation without using a holistic perspective. Instead of getting rid of unfairness, a system has been created in which people turn on each other like enemies and are always trying to sue each other for gains. This promotes a lack of sharing, distrust, a lack of ability to solve disputes through communication, greed, and envy. It is not a solution at all, it is not looking at the bigger picture, is it not taking into account the whole.

Another good example is using jail as a punishment and deterrent to crime. There is the problem of crime, and then the narrow minded threat of caging people to stop it. This causes so many other problems that it is hard to grasp. It causes people to lie about what really happened so as to avoid being caged in prison, it causes people to escalate minor disputes into serious conflicts in attempts to avoid responsibility, or it escalates minor events such as gossip into huge life changing dramas which take years to resolve, it causes a culture of blame and distrust, it causes people to persecute each other, it stops the possibility of forgiveness and reconciliation, and so on. The list is endless. The "solution" of imprisoning people isn't a solution at all, it isn't holistic. Most people try to solve problems without holistic thinking and so they just create more problems, then they try to solve those with more narrow minded small "fixes" or "band-aids" and the cycle continues. This same issue applies to problems in relationships and marriages, in businesses and friendships, and it is even true for your health, for infrastructure and for the environment. The wisdom of taking into account the whole is essential to ensuring there is harmony and unity among the parts. Always remember this whenever you run into an obstacle or a difficulty in your life.

Verse Forty One Of The Tao Te Ching

In this verse Lao Tzu speaks about how the path of the Tao seems to often be dark, obscure, difficult, changeable and even seems to lead you backwards in life. This is a crucial point to touch on, it is no doubt something which you have already thought about a lot. It seems backwards to give up attachment to the things you have worked hard to gain. It seems unhelpful, difficult, dull and pointless to practice meditation. It seems like the truths you come to understand about the Tao are all meaningless and impossible to make sense of. It might even seem like the path of wisdom is one of lowliness, poverty, or boredom, a path that everyone who is intelligent should want to avoid in life. So what's the deal? Where is the benefit in following the so called "Great way" that the Tao Te Ching talks about?

The paradoxical thing about life is that many of the truly good qualities are hard to achieve and most of the destructive qualities come easily. There are a lot of very obvious examples of this. If someone is obese then working out and eating only healthy foods is obviously greatly in their benefit. Yet working out will likely be extremely painful and demanding, seeming like the worst thing, while eating healthy can feel like starvation or going through withdrawals from certain food addictions. But there is no one who doubts that being fit and eating healthy is better for your health. The same is true for the path of the Tao and for meditation. You will just have to trust that there will be results and that the benefits will far outweigh the earlier struggles, even if you can't initially see those results clearly. Lao Tzu wants you to take his word for it, but I think you already know this is true, for most people they simply don't foster the necessary drive or motivation, or don't begin forming these good habits and routines. Don't let laziness or avoidance ruin your spiritual progression before it really begins. Trust in your logic over your feelings. Your feelings might always be telling you to just watch some television instead of meditate, but your logic knows what is better for you. Start following your logic without hesitation, rather than waiting to get approval from your feelings!

One of the reasons that it might seem like there is nothing gained from meditation or spirituality is because you're thinking in terms of seeking gain when the path actually requires you to lose and to stop seeking. You have to give up bad habits, you have to lose bad qualities. The goal is to rid yourself of all those layers which block you from the core of your being. When you have reached the source of who you really are, that is when you will experience true freedom and the heavenly bliss of egolessness.

Verse Fifty Two Of The Tao Te Ching

Here Lao Tzu advises that we should recognise our "mother", or in other words, our origin and the origin of all things, which is the Tao. Doing this is a relatively simple process, but because beings are so immersed in the world as if they were a separate, individual person functioning in it, they have come to ignore one simple truth, which is that everything you experience is actually just a solitary experience arising in your mind. When you look at the sun, you are not seeing the sun, you are just having an image appear in your consciousness. When you look around the room you are in, you are not seeing the room, you are experiencing a dream arising in your mind. When you have a conversation with another person, you are not seeing a separate person, you are just observing various sensations like colour, shapes and sounds appear in your personal consciousness. This is the essential realisation which you must learn to be aware of if you want to understand Oneness. You are one with everything you see because everything that you have ever known has been limited to an illusion or a show experienced by your minds eye. Even when you see a great mountain far away, that is just a tiny, wavering picture showing within yourself, like looking at a painting where there is the illusion that different things appear to be far away from each other. Things appear to be far away from you, or separate from you, but it is just a convincing illusion, your entire reality is your own mind.

If you have trouble perceiving this truth, the easiest ways to expand your awareness so that you can have a clear sight of it are either to practice meditation or to simply pay close attention to your vision. Look at a single object, preferably one that is not moving so that you are not distracted. You can look at a wall, a corner, the ground, grass, a tree trunk, or any other stable thing. Stare at that object for a while paying close attention to your visual sense. You will notice that very quickly that object will start to waver and your vision will become fuzzy, chaotic, bending and flickering, as if you were looking at a barely stable mirage. This is the true nature of all things, they are all impermanent manifestations arising in your mind, fleeting and empty like the wind. You can also do this while it is dark at night, you will quickly notice that there is little difference between the darkness of having your eyes closed or open. There you go – the world which you thought you had been travelling around during your life, has actually just been a changing image in your mind, like a television screen. You are not moving through the world, the world is moving within you. This is why the Tao Te Ching advises us to block off our senses and practice meditation. It is so we can stop being distracted by the show of life and finally understand the divine origin of all things, which is within us all.

Verse Sixty One Of The Tao Te Ching

The significant teaching that I want to talk about in this verse of the Tao Te Ching is the advice from Lao Tzu that it is better to teach a person of the wisdom of the Tao then it is to give them money or advice. This teaching is similar to the saying "it is better to teach the hungry how to fish then to give them a fish". In life when people have problems or issues, such as depression or hardship, it is more compassionate for you to tell them of spiritual truth then it is to try and solve their specific adversity. A lot of people today are neglecting themselves in many ways. They neglect their spiritual progression, their health, their future, their relationships, their children, and the whole world. As long as these people remain ignorant and without access to the guiding wisdom which resides within them, then they will continue to neglect themselves and others and the world will have no chance of a bright future. The degree to which people neglect their inner problems is quiet astounding, as if they are blind to the truth of what is going on. It is like they are walking around in their homes and there are shards of glass all over the floor, when they step on a piece of glass and get cut, they simply remove that piece of glass and continue walking around without cleaning up, only to get cut again soon after. Until you address the major issue in the world, which is a lack of interest in wisdom, then there will be no end to strife and suffering.

If you want to be compassionate toward someone, don't give them a gift, give of your time and of your understanding, help them to stop neglecting their inner shortcomings. It is common today when people are socialising to avoid speaking about any controversial topics and to remain silent about any flaws they believe other people have. The social etiquette dictates that talking about the flaws of another person is considered an "insult" and if you try to talk about spiritual truth it is considered a taboo conversation topic which is not appropriate to discuss. How can people improve if we do not point out the flaws we perceive them to have? How can we progress spiritually if we all feel forced to remain silent about this all-important topic? Lao Tzu advises us that that we should not be conformists and should do what is right rather than what is expected. The greatest compassion, the greatest gift, is to speak about wisdom.

Verse Sixty Nine Of The Tao Te Ching

Here Lao Tzu talks about enemies. He says that lightly engaging in conflict and considering that you have an enemy is the worst thing that you can do, because you lose your treasure which is compassion. If I had to pick one teaching that I wanted you to remember from the entire Tao Te Ching it would be this one: there has never been a human being that was deserving of hate or resentment. There has never been a person which is not deserving of compassion, mercy, forgiveness, help and kindness. Why is this true? Because every single being is almost exactly alike, even when it comes to the qualities of their person, but especially when it comes to their core nature. People only differ due to different circumstances and conditions- that's it. If you were born in different conditions and experienced different circumstances, you could end up making the exact same decisions as your most hated enemy. To persecute another human being is essentially to persecute yourself. To refuse to forgive another human being is just like refusing to forgive yourself.

• Jesus: Love your enemies !

The idea that there are "enemies" which are deserving of ill treatment, is the single most destructive idea in our world. It is driven by ignorance, unrestrained emotions, and a lack of empathy, understanding and compassion. I want you to think back to a time that you were on the receiving end of mistreatment or resentment, or to imagine such a situation. How did you feel? Did you believe you deserved to be treated poorly? Almost always the answer is no. However, you might have hated the people who you considered enemies at the time. This is a terrible kind of hypocrisy. Many people, especially when conflicts arise, says to themselves "I want what's best for me so I will care for myself at the expense of others" and they try to use blame to excuse this greedy behaviour. It is in your great benefit to put a stop to any hate or resentment you feel for past 'enemies', to let go of blame, to forgive those who have persecuted you, to consider others as your own self, and to never be wasteful or greedy. By adopting these virtues you can clear your heart of emotional impurities. Emotional blockages such as hate, anger, fear, longing, the desire for revenge, and regret, can all create very real pain in your heart. This pain often causes people to become bitter, reactive, depressed or closed off, and most of it stems from resentment of others or their choices. If you want to feel light in your heart, let go of the idea that these feelings are justified and instead recognise that they are dire mistakes. By doing so you will more easily be able to cut these thoughts and feelings off and return to a state of presence and peace. You will also be giving the world its only true hope to change from its dark path by allowing connection with other humans to flourish in your life. Humanity in modern times seriously lacks community and connection, this inability to love and open up with each other has created a more dull and lifeless way of being that is only spreading. I know you have recognised this lifelessness. Until you allow the release of all that which is blocking your heart from true freedom you will be unable to genuinely live in happiness.

Verse Seventy Five Of The Tao Te Ching

Here Lao Tzu re-iterates one theme which runs throughout the Tao Te Ching. Which is that when the government is too meddlesome and intrusive in the lives of the people then this creates chaos and a population facing many difficulties. This is important because most people today simply are unaware of the degree to which the government is preventing a wise and free society from being possible. The level to which modern governments intrude and control their populations is outright insane, it goes much too far as they try to dictate rules on every little aspect of our lives. Governments in the modern west control the education of all children for over a decade, they control what media is allowed to be aired on media outlets, they control the market and impose hundreds of laws, restrictions and regulations on how we are allowed to sell and trade with each other, they control how we are allowed to raise our own children, they use propoganda to essentially hypnotise their populations, they control taxes, they control what land we are allowed to reside on and how much it costs to do so, they control and restrict what we are allowed to build and regulate even the materials we must use to build, they even control how we are allowed to grow and trade food, as well as what kind of speech is allowed and what kind of speech is deemed illegal.

Truly government has become so intrusive that the people have lost virtually all of their freedom and live within the constraints of ten thousand rules and regulations that are extremely limiting and often completely nonsensical. It is as if the government owns the people and the people must act as the government decides. People do not even have a chance to vote on most of the laws which exists or the chance to change them. In the Tao Te Ching Lao Tzu makes it very clear that he is against intrusive and big government, and so too should you be if you ever want to see true and quick change from the effects of a narrow-minded, cold, deceptive and destructive system.

Verse Eighty One Of The Tao Te Ching

In this final verse Lao Tzu teaches that pleasant or eloquent words are not true, and true words are not pleasant or eloquent.

This truth is even more relevant today than ever, especially when it comes to people who are in the spotlight of the public eye, because the media will gossip about everything that person says, so they feel they have to avoid saying anything controversial. This leads to an outrage culture where people no longer speak plainly, truthfully, or bluntly because they fear that they will be reprimanded or hated for what they say. People today are hyper judgemental and so this tendency to speak without authenticity and to give fake and insincere opinions has spread to nearly everyone. It is a tendency which is normal in the home, normal at schools, normal among friends, and very normal among politicians. No one feels that they are allowed to speak their truth anymore, or they have completely forgotten how. In most cases people have been giving fake opinions and conforming to what is socially acceptable for so long that they have actually come to believe all the imitative and phoney things they say. Even the way people act with their body language around others is moulded by the expectations of the masses. For those who are aware of all this insincerity it is like there is a huge elephant in the room. If you are aware of this situation you might often feel like you want to shout for people to wake up and start being and thinking for themselves.

The sad fact is that most people have been so heavily conditioned that they no longer know how to be their true selves. They cling so heavily to certain ideas and ways of being that they resemble the rigid, stiff, hard and inflexible qualities of those who are dead. To be rigid, hard and stiff is just like being a dead or asleep person. These qualities are the characteristics of an egotistical person whose mind is often so narrow that it cannot accept change. On the other hand a changeable and soft person is much more open to communication, to new ideas and contemplation, and is awake to the life-giving Tao. If you want to know your authentic self it is the same as your calm and gentle self. As Lao Tzu said earlier in the Tao Te Ching, arrogance and caring for public merit brings about doom. It is like most people are in a social prison of fake pleasant-seeming words and actions where truth is not allowed to enter. The great way of the Tao is the way of life and eternal life through the power of inner truth. You cannot become authentic or find inner truth by trying to think about these things. If you try to think about being authentic then you are as far away from authentic action as you can be. If you try to think about inner truth then you are as far away from the clarity of the present moment as you can be. The Tao Te Ching teaches to let go of the need to seek satisfaction and answers, which paradoxically is the only way to achieve fulfilment and understanding.

95705021R00019

Made in the USA
Lexington, KY
11 August 2018